About the Book

Jack and Mike Couffer, the father-and-son team who have written award-winning books about summers spent in such exotic places as the Galapagos Islands, an East African lake, and a remote canyon in Arizona, turn their writing and photographic talents to their own backyard, Newport, California's Back Bay.

This is a new printing, with previously unpublished historic photographs. The original edition was a selection of *The Junior Literary Guild* and won *Outstanding Science Books for Children* awards from *The Committee of Science Educators, The National Science Teachers Association,* and *The Children's Book Council.*

SALT MARSH SUMMER

Jack and Mike Couffer

Grey Owl Pictures, Inc./Corona del Mar, CA

Photographs by Jack and Mike Couffer

Digital Production Services by Mik and C.C. Lennartson of 360°
(e-mail: ccl@360degree.com)

All inquiries should be addressed to:
Grey Owl Pictures, Inc.
716 Marguerite Ave.
Corona del Mar, CA 92625

Library of Congress Cataloging in Publication Data
Couffer, Jack.
Salt marsh summer.
SUMMARY: Describes the wildlife of a southern California
salt marsh and the efforts of dedicated individuals to save
it and its surrounding area from encroaching "civilization."
1. Tidemarsh ecology—California—Upper Newport Bay—Juvenile literature.
2. Upper Newport Bay, Calif.—Juvenile literature. [1. Tidemarsh ecology.
2. Ecology—California—Upper Newport Bay. 3. Upper Newport Bay, Calif.]
1. Couffer, Mike, joint author. II. Title.
QH105.C2C65 1978 574.5'2636 78-18718
ISBN# 0-9674488-0-8

$14.95

To Gram, who has cleaned the mud off two generations of salt marsh explorers.

And to The Friends of Newport Bay, and most particularly to Frank and Frances Robinson, whose outraged voices seemed at first as insignificant as the peeping of small birds in the wilderness. It is a tribute to their dedication that the Back Bay has become a State Ecological Reserve where birds, beasts, and people can forever coexist in harmony.

Contents

Preface

The original edition of this book was written in 1977. Now, more than 20 years later, the outward appearance of the marsh has changed less than that of the surroundings and of the writers, all of whose features bear the inevitable reshaping of time.

But the hidden heart of the marsh—the mud flats, the life-support system upon which so many of the Back Bay creatures depend—was composed of different stuff back then. The tidal flats were made up of river silt, sand, gravel, and long-dead mollusk shells, the habitat of clams and crustaceans. Many of the same creatures still inhabit the mud, but the tidal flats today are different. Muck deposited by run-off from streets and fine-grained dirt plowed up to make way for new developments constitutes most of the fresh earthy deposits. The contrast sounds bad and is in many ways, but unlike most physical changes to the landscape brought about by human intervention, it isn't a total disaster. The populations of fiddler crabs, mollusks, and other crustaceans that thrived in the original sandy mud have declined (which may be bad news for some species such as clapper rails which are feeders on crustaceans). But due to the changed character of the tidal flats, new types of protein-rich life forms—the food source for other species—have proliferated. Worms are classic bird food. Today's Back Bay mud at the peak of its most productive time—the beginning of the fall migration when thousands of hungry shore birds arrive to stoke up after a flight of 2,000 miles—is populated by up to 1,000 worms per square foot.

I

The Dance of the Fiddler Crabs

JACK

My grandfather's cottage on the sand spit that separates Newport Bay from the Pacific Ocean was one of the first on the peninsula. In the early nineteen-thirties, when I was a boy, there were still far more vacant sandlots than dwellings on the now-congested Balboa Peninsula. On summer evenings as I lay in my bed, I could hear the crash and rumble of surf and sniff the good sweet smell of the sea.

In July and August, I spent many days tramping through the countryside that stretched away in all directions from the bay. I explored the dry, toyon-choked canyons to the east. Eucalyptus trees on the ridges made cool dark pockets for ground squirrels, deer, and coyotes. Hillsides were blotched with thickets of prickly pear which were havens for cottontails and rattlesnakes. Every year a pair of roadrunners nested in the same elderberry tree, protected from my closer inspection by an impenetrable fortress of tangled cactus spines.

Sometimes I hiked along the sea bluffs. I kept to the edge of the freshly cultivated bean fields and dug in the black earth with a stick in search of Indian arrowheads.

I identified every major feature of the countryside and designated them with descriptive, if unimaginative, names: Buck Gully, Thorn Forest, Rattlesnake Hill, Cockle Sands. The marsh I called simply, Salt Marsh.

On my hikes I often saw a species of bird or some animal behavior that was new to me; this I carefully entered into my notebook, for I was seriously training myself to be a naturalist. I read Seton and Muir and was fascinated by the biographies of Audubon and Darwin, but the most exciting person I knew was real and alive. He was an uncle who visited us often and was a keen observer of nature. Tom had been staying with us for a week when he came in one afternoon from the hills where he had been painting watercolors.

"The fiddlers are mating," he said to me. "I saw them this morning at the salt marsh. Would you like to watch them dance?"

We drove through the hills toward the back end of the bay, and on the way we saw red-tailed hawks, kites, and kestrels on the fence posts. I felt that Tom and I shared the same satisfaction in seeing these noble-looking birds of prey. A golden eagle soared overhead, wings spread like a wide dark plank hung in the sky. Sometimes bald eagles, ospreys, and peregrine falcons hunted the shores, and we watched for them.

The salt marsh where we were going was an estuary of tidal water that lay protected from the ocean by a long finger of sand. On the other side of the sand spit lay a calm bay, partially dredged in the lower portion to make channels for yachts and fishing boats and islands for homes. The Upper Bay, however, was still undeveloped, a series of wild channels winding inland.

I knew the marsh well, for I often visited it on my long tramps, but I knew very little about the fiddler crabs.

Tom told me that their habitat was limited to a belt of mud that had just the right tidal division between wet and dry. He said that the consistency and texture of the mud seemed to determine where a fiddler colony would be. Because of this delicate

14

balance between tidal flow and type of mud, fiddler colonies were found in only a few locations in the marsh. But where conditions were ideal, they throve by the thousands.

It was late afternoon when we arrived. Tom drove onto the shoulder and stopped his old car. I followed him quietly across the hard-packed mud to two flat rocks the size of apple crates. Sitting on one, he motioned me to the other and whispered, "Sit very still. In a few minutes they'll be out."

The flat all around us was dotted with hundreds of dime-sized holes. We sat so quietly that I could hear the slap of tiny wavelets lapping at the mud's edge. Soon I heard a new sound, barely audible at first, a crackling noise like someone trying to walk quietly on dry leaves. It seemed to be coming from the hundreds of holes that surrounded us.

We continued to sit so very still that I felt I must move, even if only a toe inside my shoe. Then I saw a movement on the flat and I forgot my discomfort. I hadn't been aware of their mass appearance. They had moved with great stealth until, all at once a thousand eyes were watching us. On the tip of a long stalk, from every hole, an eye watched for danger. Then, seeing no movement, each eye edged up a bit farther until another eye on a long stalk swung up beside the first. They remained half in and half out of their burrows, until, as if on signal, all the fiddlers emerged onto the tidal flat.

I picked out one crab to watch. The brown-and-gray mottled fiddler had one greatly enlarged white claw as large as the animal itself. He held this pincer protectively across his face. With his smaller claw, which seemed malformed it was so dwarfed by the other, he began to probe the mud. He picked up tiny particles of food with the little claw and fed them to the mouth hidden behind the large claw. Looking at him, I realized the origin of the fiddler's name. The small claw moving back and forth across the large one gave the impression of a fiddler sawing away across a violin.

Standing up high, the male fiddler crab swings his claw in a "come hither" gesture to beckon the nearby female.

Most of the crabs looked like the one I had been watching. There were a few, however, that had two small, symmetrical pincers instead. Lacking the grotesqueness of the other crabs, these few seemed cute by contrast. They were the female fiddler crabs, and why the unequal division between the sexes I could not guess.

Moving sideways, walking high on the tips of their pointed toes, the fiddlers gazed across the mud flat. They lived so close together that their movement seemed to give life to the mud itself. But I noticed that they did not graze freely. Each confined its wanderings to a certain distance from its burrow. The fiddlers seemed limited by some invisible boundary, a territory radiating but a few inches from the center of each hole. Each individual had his plot of land, each burrow was his house, each house surrounded by a boundary as real as the lines drawn by a surveyor with a transit. Cross the line and meet the claw of a neighbor.

A shadow passed over the flat—only a sea gull soaring lazily across the sun. The crabs panicked. With a small clattering sound of armored limbs they stampeded to their burrows. In a moment the flat was deserted. I saw that territorial rights weren't the only reason for sticking close to home. The farther a crab foraged from its burrow, the farther it must run when danger threatened, and danger was present in many forms.

From the corner of my eye I looked at Tom. He sat very still, watching intently, so I did not move.

Now I noticed scattered here and there large, broken-off claws. Some lay half-buried as if long lost. Others, apparently more recently detached, lay fresh on the surface. As I was wondering how the claws had come apart from their crabs, I saw that the eyes were watching once more. Again, the crabs warily returned to the surface.

I watched one with two small pincers. She was more conspicuously marked than the other females, and, to my mind at least, the prettiest. The background of her shell was a cream color dappled with areas of light gray, and her eyes seemed to be on particularly long stalks. When she emerged from her burrow she carried a ball of packed mud cradled in her pincers, which she placed on top of a pile of similar mud balls near her doorway. After each high tide and flooding of the holes, housecleaning was evidently required. Then the female moved off, combing the mud surface with her little claws as she tiptoed sideways. She moved beyond the usual boundary. No one attacked her. She appeared to stroll at whim, farther and farther from her burrow.

Now she approached the house of a male neighbor. He seemed to be watching her advance with interest. As she drew closer, he raised himself up until his legs were nearly erect and his body high above the ground. In this stance, holding his small claw clenched to his body, he slowly extended his great claw. Reaching far out with it, then quickly drawing it back in a sweeping arc across his face. It was a classic "come hither" gesture.

With no fiddle to play, the female crab uses her two small claws to pick up food.

She drew closer. He became excited. He gestured again, faster, seeming to beckon to her. As she passed close by he outdid himself in a flurry of excited motions. But the female did not seem to notice her admirer.

Other male crabs began to raise themselves high on straightened legs as the female strolled near them. Now a few males moved toward her, forming an encircling gallery, those at the back beckoning slowly, increasing the frequency of their gestures as she drew closer, slowing down again as she passed them by.

As if not even seeing the activity she inspired, she strolled on, pecking at the mud with her little claws, leaving behind a row of tiny tracks where her pointed feet ticked the mud.

Now six male fiddlers, abreast, moved toward her. Facing the female, the wings of the male line swung wide, forming a circle around her, beckoning wildly, each apparently trying to induce her to follow him to his burrow. She tiptoed casually toward the edge of the circle and the line parted, making way. The males outside the circle moved toward her, taking up the gesture and forming a new encircling ring. In this way the circle moved with her like a wave as she strolled through the colony.

Looking away for a moment, I saw other circles of white claws gesturing in sweeping arcs to other females.

A sound like the clicking of toy china brought my attention back. Two males were dueling with their large claws. Was this the cause of the broken-off claws, I wondered? One of the males had trespassed into his neighbor's area. Reaching out with the large claw, the defender edged toward the intruder. With a rush he crashed into the trespasser. They locked claws, twisting, one losing footing and falling back. Both quickly withdrew with sideways rushes. Now sparring, they edged again toward each other. Defender rushed in, crashing against Intruder's armor with a miniature clank. As if startled by their sudden violence, the crabs separated.

Suddenly the contest seemed settled. The two fiddlers resumed grazing as if nothing had happened. It had been far from a mortal combat. Such uncontrolled jousts did not seem to account for the lost claws.

Meanwhile, the female crab had paused in her stroll. The circle of beckoning males increased their activity, wildly waving their claws. She stood surrounded, casually feeding herself with both pincers.

Now one male elevated himself to his fullest and rushed forward to stand face to face with the female. He vigorously demanded her attention. Three sweeping "come hithers!" She stopped eating. He was making points. At least she had noticed.

He darted away, running lightly sideways through the line of other males, and disappeared into his hole.

The female, apparently unimpressed, resumed eating.

In a moment the spurned male reappeared from his burrow. He walked slowly and took a place at the back of the circle. He continued to beckon from afar, but with little enthusiasm.

The female edged toward a male crab in the circle. Doubling the frequency of his gestures, the large-clawed one rushed forward. He stood before her, wildly waving his claw. Then, as if leading the way, he ran to his burrow, tilted his rigid body sideways, and disappeared inside.

The female, the circle moving with her, walked to the threshold of his burrow. She paused—a theatrically suspenseful bit of timing—then tilted her body and followed her choice into the hole.

Suddenly a pigeon-sized brown bird with long legs appeared from the tasseled cord grass at the edge of the flats. The fiddlers stampeded. Running rapidly across the mud, the clapper rail dashed onto the flat and snatched a fleeing fiddler before it could reach its hole. Holding the pincer in its bill and battering the crab's body against the ground, the rail broke off the large claw. Then it dropped the dangerous pincer, picked up the body, swallowed it, and disappeared into the grass to wait for the crabs to come out again.

Tom and I walked back to the car. The tide had been coming in while we were watching the birds. Now it reached halfway across the mud to the rocks where we had been sitting. We got in the car and sat looking out over the darkening marsh. Tom turned on the headlights even though they weren't bright enough to penetrate the twilight. We drove toward the ocean.

"There's something new in the marsh," Tom said.

I didn't understand at first—not until we came out from behind a tall clump of reeds and got a long view of the salt marsh and the entrance to the bay.

The newcomer was moored in midchannel. The lights of the dredge barge were on for the night shift, and I could see the long hose snaking from the barge to shore, spewing out the black muck, brown water and sand of the bay's bottom, dumping it in ugly piles over the reeds.

The female (right) approaches the male of her choice.

The pump was sucking up clams and worms and sand and muck, spewing it out and filling the dime-sized holes of the fiddlers, sealing them in.

"I wanted you to see the fiddlers before it was too late," Tom said. "In a few months they probably will be gone."

"It won't be the same." I felt desolate. "Isn't there anything we can do?"

Tom shook his head. "What? Stop the march of progress? Not a chance."

Hornshells are the most conspicuous year-round residents of the mud. They feed on algae and leave tracks when they move around looking for more.

2

The Tangled Gull

MIKE

There are three ways to explore the salt marsh. You can take the old road that meanders along the east shore. There's practically no traffic since it's used mainly by bird-watchers, joggers, and bicyclists. There's a sign on the side of the road that says:

**WARNING
ROAD AHEAD
MAY NOT BE PASSABLE
OCTOBER TO MAY
BECAUSE OF DAMAGE
CAUSED BY WINTER RAINS**

It's a leftover from before they paved the road last year. I don't know why they haven't taken the sign down; it always reminds me of the way the salt marsh used to be.

The official name for the salt marsh, by the way, is Upper Newport Bay, but around here we usually just call it the Back Bay.

Even though the freeway crosses over the upper end of the marsh, and hundreds of cars go past every hour, and there are houses, apartment buildings and high-rises all around the top of the bluffs that surround the bay, the old road sign helps keep the

right atmosphere in the Back Bay. On a foggy morning with the bluff tops sealed in mist and the sounds closed in by wet fog, you'd think there was nothing but you and the birds for a hundred miles.

Another way to see the bay is to walk around at the base of the cliffs on the west side. Or you can explore the channels of the bay by boat.

Once early in the summer when Dad and I were motoring around in our dory we came close to a flock of gulls. They all took off except one. He was trying, but he wasn't having much luck. Then we saw why.

He had a piece of monofilament fishing line about a hundred and fifty feet long wrapped around his leg. He could get into the air all right, but there was a four-ounce rubber-core sinker on the end of the line that would pull him down again.

You'd think a big gull could fly carrying only four ounces, and maybe he could have once. Who knows, he might have been flying for hundreds of miles with that line and sinker before he landed in the Back Bay. But by now he was pretty tired. He'd get airborne, flapping like mad with that sinker bouncing along the surface, and it would look as if he was going to keep right on going. Then he'd turn and the sinker would swing down and catch in the water and pull him in again. Four ounces and a hundred and fifty feet of line have a lot of drag.

We tried to catch him, but somehow he always had enough steam to get away. Our dory is maneuverable and fast, but the gull would flap away just as we got close, or sometimes he'd cut inside our turning radius.

Finally he flapped across the low spit of land with the sinker bouncing over the knolls and dragging through the reeds. He landed on a channel on the far side. I could barely see him; there was no way we could get to him now. He seemed cocky—very self-satisfied that he had tricked us. Of course he didn't know we were trying to help him. It was aggravating!

I was sorry to leave the gull that way, and I decided then and there to come back and find him if I could, and have another go at helping him.

3

Flight Heroics

Our dory is typical of the type that has come to be known as the Newport Dory: high sides for stability and to take the surf, a narrow flat bottom which allows the hull to slide on rollers up and down the beach, light in weight so it can be handled under oars, and a moderate transom to take a powerful outboard. She will plane at better than fifteen knots with three people, which is as fast as one usually wants to go in a sixteen-foot boat and still come home with teeth intact, and she can easily carry half a ton of gear.

Our dory has seen some hard service and many miles. We've hauled her on a trailer to Canada for salmon, to Baja for sailfish, and she's been towed behind larger vessels as a filming workboat in the San Juan and California Channel Islands. Once her tow line caught in the screw of a big power boat and pulled out the eyebolt and half her stem, but a bit of fiberglass and paint put her right, and she's as sound today as when she was built nearly twenty years ago.

In the Back Bay she's a treat to work, with her two inches of draft when the engine's tilted up, and as a stable camera platform she can't be beat. But heading into a wind chop on the open sea, that flat bottom will pound so as to knock your teeth out if you don't slow down to a modest speed.

We trailed the dory down to the bay early the morning after we had seen the gull tangled in the fishing line. It didn't take long to find him again. He seemed refreshed after a night's rest, and flew vigorously with the trailing line and its hanging sinker. The tide was running out and he flapped down to settle among a few hundred of his kin in the middle of the mud flats. It was impossible to approach him there with the boat, and to try to wade through that goo and chase him down was out of the question.

We gave up hope of catching him for the time, but gulls became the subject of the day's investigations.

Actually we were already somewhat knowledgeable on the behavior of gulls. A few years ago, I spent many weeks photographing the film *Jonathan Livingston Seagull*, and to film gulls, you first have to study them. Most of the filming for Jonathan was done along the picturesque Big Sur coast, but parts of it were filmed right here in the Back Bay.

The first thing we discovered at that time was that gulls in different parts of the state often behave in different ways: Gulls at Big Sur often reacted completely differently than the same species at Newport.

Several sequences in the script called for shots of gulls flying in military formations. Ordinarily gulls do not fly in angular formations such as the familiar formal wedges of geese. A flock of gulls in flight it usually a random scattering of birds, all heading in the same direction, but spread out like a bunch of windblown leaves across the sky. At least that's the way the Big Sur gulls fly, and after weeks of filming I still didn't have the formation shots we needed.

But I remembered having seen gulls flying in a different way near the salt marsh. One weekend I drove home from Big Sur and confirmed my impression. These Back Bay gulls were different.

Every morning just after dawn, hundreds of gulls flew inland from the ocean where they had spent the night roosting, and headed across the Back Bay for the county dump just east of the marsh. They flew straight, fast, and almost always in formations. There were single-file lines, lines abreast, "V" formations, "U"s, "I"s, "W"s, and even "Y"s—nearly every imaginable configuration.

Only when the flock took wing and left him all alone were we able to pick out the tangled gull.

When I brought a small film crew to the Back Bay to photograph gull formation flying, I discovered a bonus. Another of the problem maneuvers we had been unsuccessful in filming at Big Sur was the aerobatic stunt called the tailspin.

At one point in the story, when Jonathan is trying to break through from ordinary flight to the extraordinary maneuvers practiced only by those gulls that live on other cosmic planes, he tries a particularly courageous maneuver, fails, and goes into a spin that carries him falling out of control through thousands of feet of sky. Even our trained gulls couldn't be induced to perform such outrageous feats, and the miraculous pull-out at the bottom of his fall precluded the use, as was suggested by someone at the studio, of an old gunnysack covered with feathers and a couple of tied-on wings.

But on the afternoon of the day we had been filming formation flying, we were in the Back Bay to film the return of the gulls as they passed overhead on their way from the dump back to the sea.

On this particular day a strong wind blew onshore and the birds circled like hawks in an updraft, gaining thousands of feet of altitude above the dump before heading seaward. These gulls had spent all day wading around through trash, dust, and garbage, and dodging bulldozers in the dump. Jonathan's idea of heaven might have been perfection in flight, but to the ordinary gull, particularly after he's spent a hot day in the dump, it's a cool bath!

As the gulls passed over the upper end of the Back Bay, they spotted the pools of clear cool water sparkling in the flats. I was glad to see that the garbage scavengers are really fastidious birds, after all. One by one the gulls peeled off from their high-altitude course and dropped toward the pools. Most of them circled slowly down to glide to smooth landings on the pools, but about one gull in ten (perhaps those with something of Jonathan's individualistic yen for speed) pulled out all stops, flipped into a spin, and dropped like a tumbler pigeon. These exceptional birds fell so fast and erratically that I was unable to keep up with many of them with my camera. Eventually, after many tries, I captured a few dozen seagull tailspins. I even filmed one particularly spectacular pull-out and recovery which, when cut into the sequence of Jonathan's fall, surely qualified that anonymous bird to the title of Supergull.

But these reminiscences of gull heroics in the past did nothing toward solving our present dilemma. What to do about our tangled friend? We still didn't have the answer, and we had to leave the gull and his problem for another day.

4

The Least Terns

Some things in the Back Bay are gone forever. Well, maybe not forever—that's a big word. Take the fossil beds, for example. When I was younger I used to love to dig in a particular gully in the Back Bay. With just a little work you could find many kinds of fossil shells, whale bones, shark teeth, and stingray jaws. The Los Angeles Natural History Museum excavated there for years and the supply of fossils seemed endless. They found between 500 and 600 different species of fossil life, mostly from the Miocene age.

But then developers built the Westbluff subdivision, and they filled that gully thirty feet deep and built houses on top of all the fossil beds.

"Look at it this way," Dad says. "The fossils are still there, just as they have been for twenty million years, buried in the earth. Those houses aren't going to be there forever. But now they effectively preserve the fossil deposits until some future time."

Considered from that angle it wasn't so bad. The houses are a method of conservation.

One day we saw an old station wagon with faded paint and a State Fish and Game decal on the door parked off the salt marsh road beside a telephone company piling. A man was standing on the roof and hammering up a new ECOLOGICAL RESERVE sign under the cable-crossing warning. He said his name was Preston Johns and he was the new junior wildlife manager-biologist. He had a friendly look and I thought right away he was someone I'd like to get to know better.

"Persistence will prevail," he said as he pounded in the last nail. "If they tear it down, there's more where this one came from."

I figured this particular sign ought to stay put forever. How many people would want to climb on the roof of their car just to tear down an ECOLOGICAL RESERVE sign?

"They'll do it," Preston said. "Don't ask me why, but they'll do it."

We met Preston Johns just at the time I was getting interested in least terns. They are called least terns because of their small size, and although they have always been a part of the salt marsh, they are now an endangered species.

The main reason they are endangered is their choice of nesting areas. Least terns like lots of open clearing without brush or grass, close to protected water where they can catch small fish for their young. Sunny salt flats or deserted stretches of sand are ideal.

Preston told us that most of the least tern nesting areas are threatened with development. One of the biggest nesting areas in Southern California has about eighty-five pairs and is located on Terminal Island in Los Angeles Harbor, where a huge development will soon be built.

Another nesting area alongside the new shopping center at the San Gabriel River mouth is being torn up by people who are using it for a motocross bike track.

But least terns still hunt and feed in the Back Bay, and a few pairs even nest on the sea beach only a couple of miles away. A few years ago the State put up a fence around the beach nesting site. This spring some of thee terns moved outside the fence and scooped nests in the sand on the public beach alongside the reserve. Preston roped off the area and put up his signs. It's a beach that surfers and sunbathers use a lot, and Preston wasn't

Preston Johns

very optimistic about being able to protect the birds with just a rope and some signs. But he's pleased with the public cooperation. He says it's an indication of the new awareness of ecology.

In order to make up for all the nesting sites that are being taken away from the terns, Preston wanted to restore some of the old sites that the terns had abandoned in the Back Bay.

Up at the end of Shellmaker Island, Preston had an experiment going. He told us about studies that had been made at the other least tern nesting areas with a metal hoop called a Raunkiaer's Circle. As a part of the study a scientist throws this hoop over his shoulder and lets it fall at random. He throws it a certain number of times in each area, and after each fall he counts and identifies all the plants inside the ring.

One biologist did this at several least tern-nesting sites. Then Preston carried out the experiment at the old, abandoned least tern nesting area in the salt marsh. He was trying to answer the same question I had been asking myself. Why didn't the least terns nest there anymore?

Throwing a hoop over your shoulder doesn't sound very scientific. But when you think about it, it's a perfectly good way to find out the average plant life of one area so you can compare it with another. It's certainly easier than just counting all of the plants in, say, five acres, and it's supposed to be statistically accurate. Anyway, they found out that there were more plants growing in the abandoned sand hills nesting area than anywhere where terns were now nesting. It seemed logical to think that the reason the terns weren't using the sand hills was because there were too many plants for their liking.

Nobody had counted the plants when the terns used to nest in the sand hills, but Preston thought that if the plants were thinned out the terns might come back to nest. So with the help of a few friends we cleared off the hills. But so far no luck.

"Well, maybe next year," Preston said. "The more pressure they get in other places, the more they'll have to scout for new sites."

There was another part of the salt marsh that Preston was investigating with the thought of improving the wildlife habitat. The very end of the Back Bay was once used by a salt-production company. The remains of old dikes and squared-off flats that were once evaporation ponds scar the area. It's been years since the company abandoned the salt works, and mud has washed into the old ponds and the dikes are broken down. The soil is too salty for plant life and it all looks dead—hardly a fit-looking place to be a part of an ecological reserve.

As they stand, the old salt flats seem to be only an eyesore. Preston and other biologists have been studying the possibility of dredging out that salty ground and creating a marsh again the way it was before. Made into marshland, it would add another 20 acres to the endangered clapper rail and Belding's savannah sparrow-nesting habitat. But wildlife management specialists have learned that things in nature aren't always as they appear to be. That's why the biologists wanted to study the area thoroughly before finally deciding to dredge. Preston said that a wetland has never been restored on the West Coast before, and there are big differences between West and East Coast marshes, so they have no one else's experience to draw on. It was good that they went slowly and didn't just start making over the salt flats, because this year, just when the marsh rehabilitation study was going full steam, least terns moved in.

It was late in the nesting season, long past the time when the last least terns should have had their chicks. Then, suddenly, ten pairs showed up at the salt flats and began making nests.

If a tern nest is disrupted early in the season, the terns will build another one and lay a second clutch of eggs, and maybe even a third if the second nest is also ruined. Preston figures these were probably birds that had tried nests at some other site *and had failed. This was probably their third attempt this season to hatch chicks.*

We were disappointed that the terns had bypassed the sand hills we'd cleared. They flew right over them every time they went up and down the bay from the salt flats to the feeding grounds. Still, we were glad to have them.

High tide on the mud flats. The greatest concentration of birds occurs in winter. By early summer most of the travelers are gone, and the rails, Belding's savannah sparrows, and least terns are alone to tend their nests.

But now the plan of dredging the entire salt flat and making it into a marsh was knocked flat. It wouldn't do to make new habitat for clapper rails and Belding's savannah sparrows and at the same time wipe out a habitat for least terns. All three were endangered species and equally important. So a new element was included in the dredging plan. Salt flat islands will be left as tern areas in the rehabilitated marsh. That way the terns will be safe on islands, the rails and sparrows will get some new marsh, and people will have something nice to look at. There will be something for everyone. It seems like a good compromise, and Preston thinks it will work.

When the terns showed up at the salt flats, it didn't really surprise the biologists. "It's funny," Preston said. "The earth has a way of looking after itself. It's always teaching us lessons. Sometimes if you leave it alone long enough, everything goes full-circle. All we wildlife and environmental managers can do is try. In this case, if we'd taken what might have seemed like the obvious first inclination and wiped out the salt flats completely, we might have been wrong. But we still can't be sure." He shrugged, then took a look of assurance.

"There's one thing we know positively. The Back Bay can't be called a natural area anymore. Man has already had a big effect on it. Construction projects miles away cause silt to wash into the drainage and eventually into the bay. Every time it rains, insecticides from agriculture and peoples' gardens, and pollutants from streets and rooftops wash into the bay. If we don't dredge the bay at all, the channels will fill up with sediments, tidal flushing will stop, and the marsh will disappear. Left alone, the Back Bay will fill up and turn into a meadow. Meadows aren't yet an endangered environment. It's the endangered environment as much as the species that we're trying to preserve. The two go together."

There have been some complaints made by people who would rather see the bay left just as it is, untouched. Preston is sympathetic to the protests. They are made by people who are on his side but don't understand all of the problems.

"Since our goal is to save the Back Bay as a marshland, it's going to force us to make some alterations," Preston said. "That's what wildlife management and habitat improvement is all about. A month ago I saw the salt flats as a barren, ugly, man-made, sterile intrusion on the marsh. Now I see it with a different perspective. Maybe the least terns will return someday to the Shellmaker Island knolls. But for now they've staked a claim to the salt pans and I'm glad they're here. When construction starts at Terminal Island and that colony of terns is wiped out, there are going to be eighty-five pairs looking for new grounds. Maybe this year's nucleus colony will attract them to the Back Bay. That's what we're hoping."

A month later Dad and I drove down the Back Bay road. The least terns were gone from the salt pans, headed south with their new broods for Mexico. Halfway down the bay we saw Preston's old station wagon pulled off by the road by the piling where we'd first met him. He was climbing down off the roof as we pulled up, a fresh ECOLOGICAL RESERVE sign newly nailed into place on the pole.

"So they did tear it down?" I asked.

"I knew they would," Preston said. "But there's more where this one came from."

With a wildlife biologist who has persistence like that, it gives us a lot of hope for the Back Bay.

5

The Photo Blind

One Christmas when I was about fourteen, I received a folding camera of a type no longer seen. Its lens gave a view comparable to looking through the bottom of a Pepsi bottle. I don't know whether or not the poor quality of my work can be excused by the camera, but my pictures were terrible. Still, it is difficult to shoot good wildlife photographs with a wide-angle lens, and I considered it a reasonable victory when I could get close enough to just identify an egret or a curlew clearly in my viewfinder. The many excellent wildlife pictures you see today are as much the result of refinement in equipment as they are the result of increased expertise in stalking animals. At least that is my excuse for my early fuzzy longshots. Mike is taking pictures now with a 400mm gunmount lens on a reflex Nikkormat that gives him a good view of a bird's eyeball at distances where I used to feel lucky to get a whole bird in the frame.

I used my first camera until the leather bellows wore out. Then I replaced it with the newest thing on the market—an Argus C3, the forerunner of today's sophisticated 35mm cameras. The things I remember most about my C3 were that, although it still had a noninterchangeable, wide-angle lens, it did have the latest type of rangefinder focusing. It also had incredibly sharp corners on its heavy boxlike frame, which accounted for the many black-and-blue bruises that seemed perpetually to mark my body at neck-strap length.

Years later I came back to the salt marsh to photograph the wildlife professionally. As I mentioned earlier, sections of *Jonathan Livingston Seagull* were also filmed here.

One year, when the least terns were still plentiful, I set up a photographic blind on the end of Shellmaker Island where two sandy knolls were being used by about a dozen pairs of least terns.

These delicate little black and white birds make their nests in the simplest possible way—just a slight depression scooped in the sand, sometimes decorated with a few broken bits of seashell.

Least terns attack intruders in their rookeries with protesting cries and rocketing dives that are cut off barely short of actual contact. But if the intruder is a photographer who hides in a blind, the terns seem to forget the stranger and quickly resume their normal activities. Some species of birds have a better memory than terns, which makes it necessary for two people to go to the blind. Once the photographer is hidden inside, the other person goes away and the birds, evidently unable to count, see the departure of the intruder and are put at ease. But such methods of deception are not necessary with least terns. They seem to react only to the presence of intruders that they can see.

For my photographic blind I brought with me a large empty cardboard box which had been used as a shipping carton for a refrigerator. Refrigerator cartons make excellent photographic blinds. First off, you can't beat the price. Appliance stores are happy to give them away just to be rid of them. Also, a cardboard carton is light and can be collapsed and folded flat for carrying, and one can quickly carve viewing ports wherever needed with a pocket knife—all desirable qualities for a photo blind. Three-sided flaps cut into the cardboard at advantageous places make perfect photo ports; when finished with a window, the flap can be closed up and sealed with tape. But because of the wind resistance of a refrigerator carton and its tendency to sail in the breeze, the bottom must be securely staked down or weighted with rocks to keep it from blowing away.

Such a carton, as you can see, is as well suited to the purpose of wild bird photography as it is to shipping refrigerators.

On this particular day of least tern filming, I had spent all morning in the blind, my legs cramped from the confinement of the carton. I took a break at noon and carried my camera back across the narrow causeway to my car, intending to return to the blind after lunch.

At that time the Back Bay was still a wild place and even the surrounding bluff tops were undeveloped, not occupied by houses and apartments as they are today. The bottoms of the cliffs were often used as backstops for rifle and pistol target practice, and any tin can or bottle on the flats, and every roadside sign was riddled with bullet holes. Anything two- or three-dimensional, living or dead, qualified as a target for the shooters, some of whom even drove the Back Bay road firing from their moving cars.

When I returned to my blind after lunch I discovered to my horror that it was punctured by about a dozen large bullet holes. It was obvious from the direction of entry that they had been fired from the road a hundred yards across the bay. To the shooter, my cardboard carton must have looked like old trash blown and dumped by the wind. There was no way he could have known that a short time earlier there had been a person—me—crouched behind a camera inside. I looked through those large round holes in the cardboard and my scalp tingled. If I had been inside when the reckless marksman had been potting at my carton, I would now be dead. I decided then and there that I'd just completed my least tern filming for the season.

6

Changes

Dad has told me a lot about the changes that have taken place in the Back Bay since he was a boy. The thing that struck me most was that thousands of certain kinds of living creatures are now rare or gone completely—like bubble shells, for example. Even I can remember when I used to collect bubble shells in the marsh. Thinking about all the changes and the vanishing wildlife had me feeling pretty pessimistic. It seemed that even if the bay was now being saved, it was probably too late.

One afternoon we went to talk to Ron Hein, who is another Fish and Game Department biologist working on the Back Bay project. He is Preston's boss, in charge of preserving the bay's ecology and making things better for the wildlife. The first thing he told us was that studies show that someday they can expect over a thousand people a day to visit the marsh. That was the most depressing news I'd heard yet. The wildness would be gone. When he went on to outline the department's plans to control all those people, it didn't sound quite so bad. At least the people wouldn't be bothering the wildlife.

Ron said that soon they would have to enforce a lot of regulations in the Back Bay in order to protect the wildlife. As it is now, people tramp around just about anywhere they want, and dogs run all over the place chasing birds, which "is not beneficial to an ecological reserve," as Ron understated it. He says that eventually everyone will have to stay on paths. I think it's sad,—it won't be nearly as much fun to go to the Back Bay. But I can understand that you can't have a thousand people wandering all over the marsh every day. All the plants would be mashed, and there wouldn't be any room left for the wildlife.

Nevertheless, I found depressing the thought of being stuck with a lot of tourists on a trail, and I told Ron.

"I thought you were looking at this Back Bay project as an optimistic sign of what's happening with conservation and ecological awareness," Ron said. "I find the protection aspects very encouraging in that regard."

But I kept thinking about paved trailways and "Keep off of this" and "Don't do that" signs. The Back Bay was fine the way it was, where you could turn over driftwood to see what was underneath, and snoop around in the reeds. "I think it's terrible," I said. "Why be optimistic, anyway?"

Ron looked at me for a long time and shook his head. "Why be optimistic? Well, hell, son—optimistic people have more fun!"

I've been thinking about it ever since he said that and he's right. It's made me feel a lot better to look on the bright side.

One day, with the good feeling of knowing that the wildlife of the marsh was going to be protected forever by the ecological reserve, Mike and I set out to take account of all there was left to preserve. There was still plenty, both in variety and in numbers, but there were some species conspicuously missing since the days of my youth.

We couldn't find more than a few specimens of either of the two species of bubble shells that used to thrive here by the thousands. And when I was a boy, the bottom side of every piece of driftwood was plastered with dozens of small olive ear shells. But now, after a whole day's search, Mike and I found only a few, which we carefully returned to the marsh. And several pieces of clams which used to be numerous are now rare or completely gone.

Can you find the tiny fiddler crab? (He's halfway between the comb and the cup.) Fiddler crabs are gone from most of the bay. One of the biggest colonies remaining is found in a backwater where the tides leave the bay's trash.

What happened to all of these mollusks? we asked ourselves.

One interesting theory has to do with the tons of poisonous copper, mercury, and other heavy metals that have been deposited in the Lower Bay. There are nearly 10,000 yachts moored in Lower Newport Bay, and a few hundred in the lower end of the Upper Bay. Our harbor has one of the largest concentrations of pleasure craft in the world. Every one of these boats has its bottom painted with special antifouling paint which keeps it free of marine growth. The basis of this preparation is poisonous copper. The binding material which holds the copper in suspension is made so that it will slowly erode away, constantly exposing a new layer of copper to living organisms, and sluffing off any marine life that becomes attached. Every boat in the bay is given a new coat of antifouling paint about every eight months.

What happens to all of that heavy copper? It falls to the bottom, where presumably it must accumulate. There must be thousands of tons of heavy poisonous copper on the bottom of Newport Bay. If the copper kills barnacles and teredos on the boats, then it must kill other bay organisms as well. Can it be that concentrations of that poison has been carried by the tides into the Upper Bay?

If not, and it lies on the bottom of the Lower Bay, constantly growing in volume, what effect does it have on the species there? And how does it affect the bottom-feeding fish and other organisms that migrate to and from the Back Bay? If this poison is an important factor in the ecology of the Back Bay, it could be a tough one to manage. No one yet has come up with an answer.

Opposite: The snowy egret, hunted to rarity during the 1920s for their plumes which were the rage as decorations on women's hats, is a common resident of the Upper Bay.

Dad and I spent one whole day taking pictures of shorebirds in the salt marsh. When we arrived early in the morning the bay was high and wavelets were lapping through the pickleweed, but by afternoon there were only little trickles in the channels where the tide ran out. Herons and egrets speared small fish that were trapped in the pools, and willets, curlews, godwits, and sandpipers flocked over the flats, sticking their bills into the mud. Once in a while one would pull out a worm or a clam and quickly eat it. I got a nice shot of a great blue heron swallowing a good-sized croaker, and some studies of avocets "combing" the shallows. Avocets feed in a very strange way: they side-skim their upturned beaks back and forth as they wade through the water. Sometimes a group of them will work side by side, cooperating to herd shrimp or little fish into dead-end channels.

We walked around until long past good picture-taking light just to watch the sunset and the birds getting ready for the night. Sunset is when the least and Forster's terns are the most active, diving and plopping into the water as though they'd been shot, but as soon as they splash they fly up again, often with little fish in their beaks.

It was late when we started home—tide was already coming back in. As we drove around a curve in a little-traveled part of the marsh, we saw a man pulled off the road with a Red-E-Rentals trailer hitched behind his car. He was just dumping the last of about a ton of trash into a beautiful area of marsh. It really made me sick—and mad, too. Dad was pretty upset himself.

Dad drove on past. Then he stopped and started to get out with his camera.

I didn't know what was going on. "It's too dark for pictures," I said. "Besides, we're out of film."

"Never mind," Dad said, and he started toward the back of the car.

I got out, too, just as the man was pitching a huge tattered sofa from the trailer into the marsh. The mud sucked it up, and it sunk halfway to the cushions. The guy was real heavyweight! He'd tossed that big sofa as though it were feathers.

Dad started snapping away with his camera, even though he knew it didn't have any film. I still wasn't sure what was going on. And I didn't like the look of the guy with the trash. He glowered at Dad and said, "What the hell's going on?"

"Just getting evidence," Dad said.

Then Dad turned to me in a loud voice, "Have you got the license number written down?"

I said, "Yeah," and we headed back for the car. We piled in as the man headed toward us.

Dad rolled down the window. "Smile," he said. "You're on Candid Camera." And he snapped the shutter a couple of more times.

The man stood looking at us. You could see he was trying to decide what to do. I thought he was going to hit Dad.

I think Dad figured the same thing. "You know there's a public dump," Dad said as he started the engine.

"It's closed," Muscles said.

"Well, it'll be open at eight o'clock tomorrow morning."

"I've got to be at work."

"Then that's your second problem," Dad said. "After the cops come to see you about these pictures." And we drove away before the man had a chance to get tough.

The next morning we went back to see if anything had happened. Just as we'd hoped, the trash was gone. Except for some broken reeds which would soon grow back and a lot of deep tracks in the mud, the marsh was clean. It would have been a great sight to have seen that fellow dragging all the trash out of the mud. At least, as Dad said, we had proved that individual action can be taken to protect the environment.

7

Enforced Wildlife

One sunny afternoon, we stopped the car along Back Bay Drive to watch a snowy egret on the hunt. He moved with that tense, exaggerated stealth of all the heronlike birds, placing one foot carefully after the other, each step calculated, all the time holding his neck on cock like a crossbow set to fire. The egret's sharp beak was drawn back like an arrow ready to launch. He stopped in water less than knee deep, which for a snowy egret is about six inches, and stood as still as a porcelain ornament. Then he did something I'd never seen before. He moved slowly ahead, and as he placed each foot on the bottom he deliberately shuffled his toes in the mud, trying to scare up hidden creatures. He did this for several steps; then the technique succeeded. Suddenly the black beak arrow shot out. Back came the beak, holding at its tip a small wiggling flatfish, probably a baby stingray or sole. We couldn't tell. The egret tossed up his head, flipped the fish, caught it so it would slide down headfirst, that is, with the spines going the easy way, and swallowed.

Long-legged waders have evolved other devious methods to help them with their fishing. I was reminded of the African wader that makes a habit of crouching low over the water and spreading its wings in a curved umbrella, making an apparent shady refuge for fish—right beneath its waiting dagger-beak.

Curlews are among the shore bird tourists that fly south to spend the winter in the sun. When spring comes they will return to Alaska to build their nests.

An ornithologist in Florida reported that one of the waders had developed an even more remarkable technique. It sprinkled bits of salvaged garbage onto the water, using it as chum to bring small fish into the range of its spear.

We drove slowly on, now rounding the curve where Shellmaker Island came into view. Suddenly, there before us, as if grown from the sand and green cord grass, was a disturbing sight. Mysterious wooden stakes with orange plastic streamers had appeared across Shellmaker Island. They were the kind of temporary monuments that land surveyors use to clutter virgin countryside before the big boys—the ones with bulldozers— move in. Ordinarily, for us, these would be flags of war.

"Better check this out with Preston Johns before you start tearing them up," I told Mike.

Later, Preston's eyes sparkled when he confronted our hard faces. He could see that we were ready to do battle. "Don't bust a blood vessel," he said with a laugh. "Those markers are only part of the vegetation study being done for the Environmental Protection Agency."

"That's a relief." Mike sighed. "We thought the wrecking crew had sneaked in overnight."

"No," Preston said. "But one morning not too far in the future, you are going to find surveyor's flags for some types of limited development."

"Oh, no!" Mike said. "Why can't they just leave the marsh alone?"

"The State has allocated over half a million dollars to con- struct a Nature Interpretive Center and trail system," Preston said. "And an elevated boardwalk will be built over a section of salt marsh so that people can be exposed to the cord grass and pickleweed environments without trampling everything down."

"That'll only be the beginning," Mike said. He was in the mood for a fight. I wished Preston hadn't brought this up now. Well, perhaps it was just as well to get it over with.

"The beginning of what?" Preston asked.

"The end."

Facing Mike's gloomy attitude once more, I had to ask myself if we were copping out by taking an optimistic point of view. By trying to be positive about what was planned for the Back Bay, were we selling out to the enemy?

Here was another wild landscape to be straight-lined and paved over for people and their machines rather than for nature. Look out, Back Bay! Here it comes: parking lots, paved foot-paths, computerized visitor/day ratios, flush toilets, regulatory signs, and traffic lights.

"It's inevitable," Preston said a bit sadly. "What's best? Footpaths where you can keep people under control? Or would you rather just let them tramp all over the place and beat the foliage into the ground? In some preserves, take Redwood Park, for example, earth compaction from countless human footsteps is a big problem. It's threatening to kill the trees the people come to see. Here it could be worse. It's easier to stomp these little shrubs and grasses into the ground than it is a redwood."

"But the Back Bay isn't an ecological reserve for people," Mike said. "It's for wildlife."

"The Interpretive Center is a compromise," Preston explained. "We need the support of the community. The original plan of private developers to make the Back Bay into a luxury marina for expensive homes would have added millions of dollars a year to the community in taxes. Wild birds don't pay taxes. That was a big argument the developers used against making this into a reserve."

Preston isn't one to dodge an issue. After all, he isn't the enemy. He loves nature, too. He looked at us hopelessly.

"I don't like to see paved trails and parking lots any more than you do. But people want to see all of these beautiful birds. They have every right to do so. We are planning the development carefully so that an absolute minimum of damage to the natural environment will occur.

"It's one thing to tear apart a wild place to destroy it, and quite another thing to tear it up a bit with the ultimate objective of enhancement. There's a basic difference of philosophy.

"Oh, we could just put up a big high fence around the bay and close it off to everything but wildlife. Maybe we would have to do just that if the wildlife wasn't compatible with human visitors. But that isn't the case. These birds, as you can see, quickly become used to cars and people. And the more people who come here and enjoy the birds, the more support we get for this and other similar reserves. To cut the people off would be very damaging in that respect. Since we don't want to keep the people out, we have to control them. That means some development."

I had to admit that in spite of Preston's persuasive arguments, my optimism was undermined. Not that I didn't agree with him that the compromise made sense. More than that—I saw that compromise was the only way. Perhaps that was the very problem that was nagging me, the inevitability of it.

"People management," as Preston called it, was the least of all possible evils. One had to be a realist. The Back Bay can never be again a wild, unpeopled place. It simply isn't possible because of its geographic location in the midst of hugely exploding human population center.

But the problems that Preston put forward continue to trouble me. Is this place we love so much an example of what all national parks and wildlife reserves will someday be? Only fenced-in plots of semiwildness? Expanded zoos? Botanical museums out-of-doors? If people keep multiplying and pushing on into the wilderness, I'm afraid it's the only way.

*　　*　　*　　*

The Upper Newport Bay Nature Preserve

One of the rules of the ecological reserve is that no dogs are allowed to run loose. The reasons are pretty obvious, especially during nesting season.

Dad and I were watching the birds with binoculars from the bluff top one Sunday afternoon when a large, expensive-looking car pulled off and stopped on the shoulder of the Back Bay road. A well-dressed woman let her dog out to do what dogs always have to do. There was a large flock of gulls on the flats, and a pair of the most excitable of all birds, black-necked stilts, were also nesting in the area. As soon as they saw the little dog, the stilts took off, flying back and forth over the dog, diving and landing and taking off again, the sky ringing with their cries.

It was the sort of little dog that is also very excitable, and as soon as he'd done his business the dog tore out across the pickleweed, barking and chasing the birds.

The woman watched him run for a while, seemingly amused by her little white birddog. I guess she thought it was cute. But then she saw the mud ahead. The tide was out and the mud was black and gooey. That little dog was game, you had to give him that. On and on he went, deeper and deeper into the goop, farther and farther from the car where the woman was calling "Billy! Here, Billy! Come back! Come here, you naughty dog!"

But Billy didn't seem to hear. This was probably the most fun he'd ever had.

Finally, in the midst of the mud flat, Billy stopped, completely bogged down and helpless. He stood there up to his neck in the muck and barked for rescue.

Should we or shouldn't we? I looked at Dad and he had a sort of twisted smile on his face.

"If he's still stuck out there when the tide starts in . . . ."

I knew what he meant, and I realized there was plenty of time before then. Besides, it was a long way down the cliff, and we really hadn't come to spend the day wading around through the mud to rescue a dog that shouldn't be there in the first place. I could think of lots of reasons for not hurrying right down.

The woman finally saved us from any temptation toward gallantry. She set out to rescue Billy herself.

Halfway there she was up to her knees in mud. Three quarters of the way she was in nearly to her hips. At this point slogging was getting really difficult. You could tell because she was lifting one foot at a time with her hands, pulling it up out of the sticky stuff and placing it ahead. Her shoes were left somewhere behind, sucked down to the bottom with the worms.

As she got closer, the dog tried again to free himself. Her efforts to save him must have spurred him to try harder, because now he began to bark and flounder and make some headway through the mud. In another few steps the woman was going to be stuck, too, and I was starting to figure out what we were going to do about rescuing her. Just then the little dog made a special effort and came lunging to her. He leaped into her arms and kissed her face. I doubt if she was kissing him back. More likely cussing him.

Billy's impact caused her to start to topple over backward. She was off balance, and she couldn't move her feet to catch herself, anyway. You could see it coming a mile away, and sure as anything, down she went.

Dad and I were trading off the binoculars as fast as we could. I had them when she landed spread-eagled on her back in the mud with Billy sitting on her chest and licking her face. Finally she rolled over so she could push herself up, which just about made the mud plastering complete.

She was all right. She wasn't about to drown in the mud or anything. I felt sorry for her. But perhaps not as much as I should. If that sounds mean, look at it from the birds' point of view. Too many times we had seen people letting their dogs chase the birds. It was a classic example of poetic justice, so why should I spoil it with guilt feelings?

By the time the woman had floundered back to her Cadillac, a couple of other cars, a few bicyclists, a Moped, and six joggers had gathered to watch. But none of them ran out into the mud to help. One jogger did take the lady's hand and drag her up the bank.

She was slime from head to foot. I knew from previous experience that she smelled like a sack of rotten bait. She put the dog down on the road, went to her car, and pulled out a cloth. She wanted to wipe some of that mud off the dog before she let him in. But she made one more mistake. She left the door open. Billy jumped into the open door, hopped over the seat into the back, and shook. It was like a bomb going off. Mud exploded inside the car. We could hear her screech all the way to the bluff top: "Billy! How could you?" Then she flung herself into the driver's seat, mud and all and sped away.

The trail she'd gouged out and back through the muck lasted through at least a week of tides, and every time I saw it I nearly fell off my bike laughing. I wonder if she ever got the mud or the smell out of her car?

8

Shrew

When I was about ten years old I went through a turning-over-rocks phase. I loved to see what was on the underside, and the bigger the rock, the more likely it was to have something beneath. I guess it was the spirit of a treasure hunt that intrigued me, combined with the thrill of possible danger (I turned up enough rattlesnakes, scorpions and giant centipedes).

Dad lectured me many times about disrupting the environment, but I was seriously addicted. I didn't want anything more out of it than just a look underneath, and it finally seemed to satisfy him when I promised not to kill the rattlesnakes and to always return a boulder to its original bed after I'd had a peek. At least we eventually compromised on that solution, even though I knew he still disapproved.

There is a wild hillside and a small bushy canyon in the hills near the Back Bay where I used to indulge in my rock-turning habit. For years there has been talk of putting a freeway through there, and if not, it's sure to be ripped up for a housing development before long. At the moment the plot, part of the Irvine Ranch, is wild, but it doesn't have much future, so I suppose in the long run my turning stones there didn't have much ecological effect.

But at the time my compulsion was most intense, the Irvine guards made it even more adventurous. They patrol the area in Jeeps, and their Jeeps have a special green-and-white paint job so you can spot them far off, which is a serious disadvantage to the guards when it comes to catching kids. But just toward the end of my stone-turning days, the city police started helping out the guards with their helicopter. The hills they were trying to keep us out of were mostly open grasslands, but in the canyons and on most steep hillsides there was enough brush to dive into when the chopper appeared. The choppers had a way of suddenly zooming up from behind the crest of a hill and swooping down on you, though, and once spotted there is no escape.

In all my years of infiltrating the Irvine Ranch land the Jeep guards hadn't caught me more than two or three times. Then came the chopper. After that my stone-turning life went downhill. They got to know me so well they called me Dan'l Boone, and I guess they pretty much gave up on rehabilitating me.

Once when I was hiding in a thicket with the Irvine Jeep stopped on the ridge only a few feet away, I heard the guard talking to the police on his radio. "It's only Dan'l Boone, again," he said. "And he's made it into the bushes. I'll see you back at the base." Then he drove away.

It all seemed a bit too easy, so I stayed put. About ten minutes later the helicopter came roaring over the ridge like he was on a low-level strafing run with the Jeep thundering along right beneath him. They must have thought they could smoke me out with such simpleminded deception. They didn't get me that time, but there were occasions when you just had to cross the fields to get from here to there, and then you were a sitting duck.

One day Dad wanted me for some important reason and went through the fence looking for me. He'd been pretty good at ducking the Jeeps, too, but he didn't know anything about the chopper. They caught him in the open and held him on a hilltop, hovering overhead and bellowing at him over their loudspeaker to stay where he was as though he'd been caught red-handed at armed robbery. I can tell you, it's terrifying to be all alone with the propwash of that whirlybird beating down on you, with all of the racket and the squawk box telling you to "lie down on the ground and spread your arms," or some such overlydramatic command. I was watching the whole thing from up in the branches of a tree and I could sure sympathize with Dad.

Pretty soon the guard in the green-and-white jeep arrived. This was the one who wore the ten-gallon hat and the pearl-handled revolver, and I knew Dad was in real trouble.

The guard figured out somehow that Dad was Dan'l Boone's father, and he jumped on the chance to make a big example. He was double-tough. He wrote Dad a citation for illegal trespass and he also wrote him up for entry into an area closed because of extreme fire hazard. That was ridiculous since we'd just had some heavy rains and the hills were green. But the fire hazard signs were still up. He did that so Dad couldn't just mail in a check, but would have to appear in court. So Dad had to spend all day in court waiting for his turn; then the judge fined him thirty-five dollars and put him on probation. He also gave Dad a long lecture and did his best to humiliate him. Somehow Dad's experience dampened my own urge to play games with the guards, and since then I haven't turned many stones on Irvine land. But at the peak of my career, I knew every good flat rock over an area of many acres and I had turned them all many times. I knew just which ones were most likely to have a mouse nest under them, a tarantula, or a rattlesnake, and I even fixed up some rocks that originally were deeply embedded in the soil by propping them up with little pebbles to make better dens. I wasn't damaging the habitat, just peeking in.

I found some rare things, too. Like the worm snake. Worm snakes aren't supposed to be in this area at all, and the species doesn't even appear on the checklist of animals that the

Department of Fish and Game made for the ecological reserve. Neither does the rattlesnake, but everyone who has been around these hills knows that there are two species of rattlesnakes and they are quite common.

But my worm snake was very rare. I found him in a nest of little black ants and brought him home for positive identification after which I planned to take him back to his stone. But Dad wanted to show him to the curator of reptiles at the museum, so we took him to Los Angeles. Then the curator said that he'd like to have him for the museum collection, and even though Dad and I both had reservations about it, we let him stay there. Now he's in a jar of pickle and stuck away on a shelf. Well, as I said earlier, none of the animals in these hills have much future, anyway. I should have taken him down to the ecological reserve and let him go there. But there wasn't an ecological reserve at the time, and it's as much forbidden to let anything go there as it is to take anything out.

My other rare find had a better fate.

One afternoon I turned a favorite stone in the area I called Rattlesnake Rockpile and a little animal darted out. I barely saw it—just about a flash—but I knew right away it wasn't an ordinary mouse. It was about mouse-sized, and mouse-colored, but it didn't move the same.

Anyway, I pounced and grabbed it. Sure enough, it wasn't a mouse. I'd never seen anything like it in the flesh before, but I knew right away from pictures I had seen that it was a shrew.

Well, to catch a shrew might not seem at all unusual. But these hills in Southern California are dry, semidesert, and not the damp forest kind of place where shrews are usually found.

I brought my catch home, fixed up a terrarium with some rocks and sand, and had a good look at him. Dad got out the books, and here's what we read in H. E. Anthony's Field Guide to North American Mammals:

> *Crawford Shrew or Gray Shrew.* Notiosorex crawfordi. *A small Shrew with conspicuous external ear, relatively short tail, and slender body. Olivegray; trail above like back, below like underparts. Underparts whitish. Total length, 3.6 inches; tail vertebrae, 1.24 inches. Distribution from eastern Texas to southern California, thence southward to the cape region of the peninsula of Lower California.*

That was my shrew, all right. The gray shrew, also sometimes called the desert shrew. But what the book said next was the most interesting:

> *The Gray Shrew is the rarest of the North American Shrews. Unlike the other members of the family, it lives in dry regions and not only does it appear to be rather local in its distribution, but also exceedingly scarce in the regions where it is known to occur. The capture of one of these mammals is a noteworthy achievement, and any collector who secures data on the life history of this little known creature should earn a niche in the Mammal Hall of Fame.*

Now that was exciting news. Even if the last statement was a bit exaggerated—even if there was a Mammal Hall of Fame, which I very much doubt.

Still, I had a rare live gray shrew and a chance to study it.

The first thing I did was name him. I couldn't think of anything better, so I called him Shrew. Then I tried to feed him. He belonged to the group of animals called insectivores, so it was pretty obvious what he ate. I went out in the yard and collected samples of every bug I could find. He almost talked to me by the way he showed his preference for the different bugs I offered. Runners, no; slugs, no; pillbugs, no; flat sowbugs, yes; earwigs, okay; crickets, a very big YES! Definitely! He practically hollered "please" the way he went for crickets.

And he was no slouch when it came to quantity. Shrew kept me busy turning stones and catching bugs.

I kept him in the garage where there was lots of activity, and in a few days he grew very tame, always coming out when someone was in the garage and looking for food.

During the months that Shrew lived in the garage, our cat caught two other gray shrews and brought the carcasses to the doorstep. They were the only shrews she ever brought home—and both while Shrew was living in the garage. We wondered if they were drawn to us by Shrew's presence? Of course our cat could have caught them far off in the hills and brought them home, or it could have been the peak of a shrew cycle, or it could have been coincidence. I guess we'll never know.

When I had Shrew for a few weeks, I decided to try some more experiments with him on different foods. After all, if I was going to earn a niche in the Mammal Hall of Fame, I had to make some scientific studies.

I found he practically did handsprings for black widow spiders. He attacked scorpions without hesitation; the first thing he did was bite off their stingers. He knew exactly what he was doing. He loved centipedes, the bigger the better. He went for them at the head. Some of the larger centipedes I gave him had big mandibles that could have snipped his little foot off, but he darted in and out like a mongoose after a cobra, and soon had a

Shrew dining on a centipede.

centipede twice his size by the head and was eating his way down to its tail.

He was a game little hunter, and I never got tired of watching him go for insects. But catching all of those bugs got to be a time-consuming project. And I couldn't miss a day.

The books said that shrews have such a rapid metabolism that they'll starve to death if they don't eat every day. I don't know if it's true or not, but I didn't take any chances and fed him daily. Maybe it was all that stone-turning in search of Shrewfood that finally slackened my habit. We even took trips to the mountains and tore old rotten stumps apart to gather live termites, and carried them home by the gallon. That way I didn't have to roll stones and dodge the green jeeps every day.

Dad has a friend, Bill Woodin, who is director of the Arizona-Sonora Desert Museum, which exhibits only living animals from that geographical area. Dad learned from Bill that the museum had never exhibited a desert shrew, even though it was an animal that was found within the area they specialized in, because they'd never been able to catch a live specimen. So I volunteered to donate Shrew. During Christmas vacation we drove him over to Tucson and saw that he was set up in fancy quarters with a sign calling attention to his rarity.

Shrew died a few months later, and the museum published a special paper about him in a scientific journal. The only other gray shrew whose lifespan was known lived for one year, two months, and thirteen days. Shrew lived in captivity one year, three months, and seven days. He broke the record. Maybe it was all those nutritious centipedes I fed him.

I'm still waiting to be named to the Mammal Hall of Fame, but I'm not holding my breath!

Going on the assumption that the more you can look like a mud worm, the more wildlife you'll see, Mike tests the theory.

My first introduction to the gull world was my friend, Jonathan Livingston Seagull, a trained bird my dad used in making the movie.

9

The Still Tangled Gull

Every time I saw a sea gull in the Back Bay I wondered if it could be the one we'd seen dragging the fishing line and sinker. Somehow I began to identify with that gull and to think of him as something special to me. But weeks went by, and I never saw him. I supposed he'd either tangled the line in a bush and died of starvation or had broken it off at last and flown away.

Then late one afternoon as I was riding my bike home, watching the windows of houses along the bluff top flashing in the setting sun, I noticed a flock of gulls along the shore take off. One stayed behind, and once again I thought of my friend.

I ditched my bike in the reeds, worked my way closer, and sure enough, it was our line-dragging bird—still alive after all. How he'd kept that monofilament from catching on something and tying him down is anybody's guess.

I watched as he hobbled along the shore. A hundred feet behind him the lead sinker dragged a furrow in the mud. I saw my chance. If I could get in position ahead of him and hide in the reeds, it would be a piece of cake to run out a few steps and grab the line after he'd walked past.

Trying to find the tangled gull from among all of his kind seemed a hopeless task.

It took me maybe half an hour to crawl down along a low spot between the reeds where water runoff from the road had gouged a gully through the mud. By the time I got to the edge of the reeds where I hoped the gull might pass, I smelled worse than a dead fish. I could hardly stand myself, and I'm pretty used to all kinds of dirt and stink. Still, there was nothing else to do but crouch there in the mud under the reeds and wait.

When I finally got into position and eased myself up to have a peek, I saw the gull still there where he'd been when I'd started my crawl—in fact, if anything, he had moved in the opposite direction.

I knew the gull couldn't see me, yet he seemed to know I was there. I'd swear he was staring at my reeds more than at any other reeds.

Well, I figured, it's going to be night pretty soon. If I just wait, maybe I can sneak up on him in the dark. So I lay there in the mud, smelling myself and thinking about what I was going to say about being out so late, and what Dad would say, even if I did rescue the gull. In spite of all the hassle I knew I was in for, it did seem worth it.

Then, just as it started to get dark enough for my new plan to work, the gull started to walk down the flat toward the water. He reached the edge and kept right on going, swimming now, and anybody could see that he was headed for that broken piece of old liferaft pontoon that was stuck in the mud halfway across the bay.

Sure enough, he crawled up on it, ruffled and then smoothed his feathers, and settled down for the night. There was no way I could get out to him now without a boat. So I went home in my stinking muddy clothes and faced the music. That gull was getting to be a definite bother!

10

Worms!

There's a whole different life across the sandbar peninsula that separates the wave-washed ocean beach from the quiet bay. On a sunny summer Sunday there may be 15,000 people crowding the beach and riding the surf on the ocean side, while only a few joggers, cyclists, and birdwatchers visit the Back Bay.

There is also a vast difference in animal life on the opposite sides of the peninsula. The living conditions are totally different. Many species that are common on one side are not found at all on the other. You never find sand crabs, which live by the millions in the surf-washed sand, in the Back Bay—just as you never see a fiddler crab on the ocean beach. Different species of shellfish live in each environment; most species of clams, for example, choose one side or the other.

Seaside animals often seem more vigorous and tougher than their bay-dwelling counterparts. They've got to hang onto boulders through the pounding of winter storms, or survive grinding sands and crashing surf. The surf mussel and the bay mussel are closely related species; their similarities readily apparent, yet so are their differences easily seen. The surf variety hangs on to rocks and to one another through the pounding of the most violent storm waves. They have thick shells and filamentous attachments as strong and tough as nylon threads, while the mussels of the bay have thin shells and are only lightly anchored in the mud.

Even birds, which could if they wished cross quickly from one habitat to the other, have a favorite side. One rarely sees a Heermann's gull in the Back Bay, even when flocks of thousands are on the sea, and the demure black-headed Bonaparte's gull is also much more a bird of the ocean.

Plants and animals that live along the rocky ocean shore must cling tightly for survival.

One group of birds that has representatives on both sides of the peninsula is the sandpiper. Of all the species, my favorite is the sanderling. Sanderlings are birds of the surf line and waveswept sands. Their food of small crustaceans is probed from the sand on the back side of a receding wave. With legs that seem to work at double speed, they race up and down between the combers, running to probe the sand behind a lipping wave, then dashing back up the beach just ahead of the next rushing wash.

Back Bay counterparts of the sanderlings are legion—knots, dunlins, willets, and dowitchers; least, semipalmated, and western sandpipers. From September through April the flats are alive with birds, a vibrant tide of life that flows in conjunction with the coming and going of the sea. The roosting knolls and terraces are above high water, and there the flocks congregate to await the outgoing tide. When the sea is out. Leaving the nourishing mud flats bare, they come in their thousands. Flying with only their dark side visible, a compact flight of peeps is nearly unseen; then as the flock changes direction, the bright white undersides catch the sun for a dazzling moment and the entire flock flashes in an explosion of light. There's something thrilling about the flashing of a flock of peeps, an exuberance, a vivid declaration of life.

Then the flock settles as one onto the flat, immediately becoming lost among the other flocks already there, shorebirds of many sizes, all heads in common bobbing quickly up and down as long bills, short bills, curved bills, and straight bills probe the mud for food.

We noticed, spaced here and there among the busy shorebirds, a line of yard-square metal frames with wire sides and top, obviously a biological experiment of some sort. Hoping to learn about their use, we kept an eye out for the person responsible

Opposite: Millicent Quammen pulling in a beach seine.

76

for them. One day we saw someone sloshing through the mud in rubber boots, returning from the frames.

It wasn't until the figure in muddy jeans and floppy jacket was close that we realized it was a girl. We introduced ourselves and announced our interest in her project. She said her name was Millicent Quammen and she had similar studies going on at other marshes. We recalled that Preston Johns had mentioned a food-resource study. We should have put that clue together with the cages.

By fencing the birds out of an area and observing the long-term difference between the grazed and nongrazed mud, Millicent could calculate the effects of shorebird feeding on the habitat. The structures which we had called cages were not meant to keep anything in. They were there to keep birds out. She called them exclosures. Enclosures keep things in—exclosures keep things out. Only under Millicent's wire nets could one see what life would be like here without the predatory top of the food chain. My God, without the birds, it would seem that worms would take over the earth!

As far as Millicent has been able to determine, the main diet of Back Bay shorebirds is small polychaete worms. As a standard for comparison she studies samples of mud four inches square by three fourths of an inch deep. Random samples of this size are taken from both inside and outside her exclosures; she has found that in October, shortly after the migratory shorebirds have arrived, the count is about even at 500 worms for each sample. As the winter goes on, the gap between the number of worms outside and inside the exclosure widens. Then, in June, after the shorebirds have migrated away from the mud flats, the

Opposite: We took a fish sample with the seine, a part of Millicent's study. The waters of the Back Bay teem with life. Three hauls of the net produced over 500 small fish. Millicent identified and measured each, then released them back into the bay.

numbers of worms inside and outside the exclosure is again about the same. The count in any one of her samples during June, the peak of the worm season, is about 1,000 worms per sample. We were amazed. Imagine! A thousand worms, ranging in size from one-eighth of an inch to half an inch in length, in a glob of mud that would barely fill a coffee mug!

The reproductive rate of these worms is so rapid that even thousands of feeding birds don't seem to deplete the supply from one year to the next. During the height of the shorebird feeding season, the worm population is reduced by about half. But as soon as the birds migrate away, the worms quickly recoup their losses.

I told Millicent that I had observed a change over the years in the mud, from the more sandy, fiddler crab habitat of ten years ago to the present gooey consistency. She knew about the change but had no measurements of its previous state to offer a comparison between lifeforms then and now. That is a part of her reason for making studies at other marshes. Her opinion, which she is careful to point out is not yet proven by her findings, is that the change in mud has benefited the birds by making a "wormier" climate. But until she screens more mud, counts more worms, and studies more shorebird feeding habits, her ideas are only speculation.

Maybe it's one of the strange ironies of nature that situation which damaged the habitat for mollusks and fiddler crabs has perhaps ameliorated it for shorebirds. Until Millicent's studies are completed she will make no definite statement.

But there is one positive declaration that I believe I can make with Millicent's approval—the mud may or may not have changed the shorebirds, but it sure is good for the worms!

11

Crab Salad

I have always been fond of crab salad. I used to fish for rock crabs down at the jetty at the mouth of the bay. The sea constantly surges and swirls between the boulders of the jetty, making mysterious hissing and gurgling sounds from caves beneath the rocks. It's a good habitat for many kinds of marine life, and a great place for crabbing. You can climb over the boulders clear out to the navigation light on the end if you want to, but most of the big rock crabs are close in to the beach. There are several good crabbing holes, wide gaps in the rocks with sandy bottoms and deep water, where you can get a line down.

I started out rock crab fishing with a regular hook and hand line baited with fish heads. Later on I made up some wire crab rings about a foot across the crisscrossed net and the bait tied in the center. I would drop this ring to the bottom on a hand line, and then when a crab got onto the net and settled down to eat the bait, I'd pull up fast, and he'd get his legs tangled and up he'd come. I set half a dozen nets at the best crab holes and then just made the rounds, pulling nets, taking out crabs if there were any, and rebaiting. You have to leave a net down about fifteen minutes; then if the fishing is good, you usually have a crab.

The best eating parts of a rock crab are the claws. It seemed such a waste to take home a bucketful of big crabs, kill them, take off the claws, and throw the dead animals away. That bothered me. Then I thought of a possible solution.

Regeneration. Crabs can grow new limbs, I read in a book by Sam Hinton called Seashore Life of Southern California. I learned that "If the large claw [of a fiddler crab] is lost in a fight or other accident, the small claw will become the larger one at the next moulting, at which time a small one will appear in the place of the lost big one."

If fiddler crabs could do it, why not rock crabs? I went on to read more about regeneration.

> "All starfish are good at regenerating lost parts, but this one [variable starfish] is perhaps the champion. If it loses an arm, it sets about growing a new one immediately. Meanwhile, the lost arm itself may start to grow another starfish, and will be a complete animal in a few months. This new starfish is, of course, quite asymmetrical, with one very large arm and four buds; as if to even things up, the large arm will break off, leaving a stump more nearly equal to the other arms — and the cast-off portion will start the whole process again. This will continue until, after four or five 'generations' the original arm is down to about one half inch long; after that, it stays put."

That made me remember a story Dad told me about some oyster fishermen. Starfish eat oysters. These particular fishermen decided that the starfish were predators (they took the definition that a predator is something that eats what man wants to eat), and they set out to do something about it.

The oyster fishermen devised a kind of starfish catcher that was a heavy crossbar with a bunch of mopheads tied onto it. When the fishermen dragged their catcher along the bottom, the mop strings slid over the oysters but caught on the starfish and they hauled them up by the dozen.

Then, to get rid of the starfish, the fishermen chopped them up into pieces and threw them back in the sea. Every piece made a new starfish, of course, and soon the fishermen discovered that they'd just put themselves out of the oyster business.

Well, I found out what I wanted to know about regeneration. If I'd take the claws off the live crabs and then let them go, they would grow new claws and I could catch them again. But what about the crab? He had those claws for a good reason. Could he live without them? How could he eat? Well, if a fiddler crab could get along with one claw and grow a new one, why not a rock crab? If I'd only take one claw and let the crab go, he'd probably survive, too. A day's crabbing only produced half as much to eat, but it was a lot more fun.

I spent a couple of Sundays catching rock crabs and taking only one claw. Then I stopped for a while. The next time I went crabbing, sure enough, I found lots of crabs that had one big claw and a new smaller one growing in place of what had once been my crab salad.

12

Birds Forever

The light-footed clapper rail isn't the most beautiful bird I've ever seen. They look something like a small brown chicken with a longish, slightly downcurved bill, and they seem to have a scared look on their faces.

They are very shy birds, but if you want to see them, and you're stealthful and patient, it isn't too hard to find clapper rails in the Back Bay. They are fairly numerous. So are Belding's savannah sparrows, another endangered species. If there are plenty of them, you might ask, how can they be endangered?

It's because clappers and savannah sparrows are so choosy about where they live. It's their habitat that's endangered. These birds aren't adapted to survive anywhere but salt marshes; if the salt marsh goes, so do they. Nobody's out waging war against savannah sparrows or clapper rails, but if their habitat isn't protected the birds will disappear. That's already happened to most of the salt marshes in Southern California and is one reason why it's so important to protect the Back Bay.

There are other characteristics about clappers that make them distinctive in spite of their ordinary looks. Parent birds work together incubating and brooding their young. Other birds also do that, but clappers are among the few that have multiple nests.

A pair builds one nest for incubating the eggs and several other nests in the same vicinity for brooding the young after they've hatched. The incubation nest always has a bower of grass or reeds pulled over it as if to make it more difficult to see or perhaps to protect it from the sun. In addition to the incubation nest, there may be as many as four or five brood nests and these, although they are also well hidden in the cord grass, don't have the bower.

Another interesting thing about clapper nests is that they float. The nests are built on the ground in the densest cord grass, often in old tumbleweeds that have blown into the bay and become bogged down in the mud. The nests, made of woven grass stems and hollow reeds, sit on the mud, but when high tide comes they float up like rafts to keep the eggs or babies dry. The parents even make special provisions to keep the nest from floating away—the nest is loosely woven around upright stems of stiff cord grass. The moored nest slides up and down on the stems like a floating boat dock that rides on pilings.

Because they are an endangered species and would have been wiped out completely in this area if the real estate developers had had their way, clapper rails were strong ammunition for the Save the Newport Bay Committee when they were working on the state to make the marsh into a reserve. Only last month the clapper rail was in the headlines again. The Sanitation District planned to put in a new sewer line through the clapper area. They were turned down cold, even though it's going to cost the county quite a bit more to reroute the sewer.

The clapper's voice is a sharp, metallic-sounding bink, bink, bink, repeated many times. Ron Hein says the best way to imitate it is to clink two half-dollars together.

One day I heard this sound coming from a patch of reeds, so not having a couple of half-dollars in my pocket, or even one, I picked up a couple of rocks and clicked them together a few times. No answer.

The Newport Upper Bay is home to more endangered clapper rails than any other southern California marsh.

I pulled out my knife and hit it against a stone. It made a more metallic sound, a better clapper communicator. The clapper must have thought so, too, for he clapped at me and I clapped back at him. We conversed in this way for a while, but I couldn't tell you what was said!

When I was a boy there were two commercial enterprises at work in the Back Bay. In addition to the long-established salt works with its acres of solar evaporation ponds in the upper end of the bay, the arrival of the dredge barge heralded a new industry. The purpose of the dredge was threefold: to deepen the channels, to build up the islands and shores, and to excavate sea shells. Shellmaker Industries on the large island was soon excavating tons of mollusk shells. As the suction hose pumped up the bay's bottom, hundreds of years' accumulation of sea shells was sorted out. The pile grew to enormous proportions, accumulating more rapidly than the shell could be ground up, sacked, and sold as an additive to poultry feed.

I had already seen a lot of change come to the salt marsh when, a few years ago, I was approached by a woman in our community who was helping to form a committee to protect the Back Bay. This whole area, which a few years before had been known only to a few birdwatchers, biologists, and stingray fishermen, was on the threshold of becoming the biggest marine-oriented development in Southern California. She told me that the owner's master plan for development had won the tentative approval of the County Planning Commission and that unless action was taken at once it would be too late.

I wrote the lady off as an eccentric do-gooder who had a worthy cause but no chance of accomplishing anything. The obstacles to be faced from government and industry were insurmountable.

The Irvine Company, large and politically powerful land developers in a county with the fastest-growing population in the whole United States, was the owner. This was their prime land; its potential as home sites and yacht moorings amounted to millions of dollars. Change that course for the benefit of a few birds? No way. I remembered the fiddler crabs and my uncle Tom's pessimism. You couldn't stop the "march of progress."

Besides, blueprints for dredging channels and creating building sites were already drawn and approved by the city, county, state, and Army Corps of Engineers. Engineering had already been done for concrete seawalls, docks, roads, lots, sewers, sidewalks—the whole urbanization package. It was to be a water-oriented suburbia with straight cement-walled channels and close-packed houses. The adjacent Lower Bay had already been changed years ago from a wild salt marsh to expensive real estate. I felt that any effort spent trying to change the future, as much as I hated it, would only be a disappointment and a waste of time, a hopeless exercise in frustration. Thus, I declined the woman's invitation to join her committee.

To my surprise, the committee was able to pull off an incredible coup. By obtaining publicity and stirring up public response, by proving the greater value and uniqueness of the area as a wildlife refuge rather than as another subdivision, they were able to help arrange land exchanges and purchases by the State. The area is now a state ecological reserve and, except for the limited amount of commercial tourism that we realized was an inevitable and necessary compromise, the marsh is protected from development forever. An extra irony is that over a million dollars designated by the state for use in building the visitors' center and making habitat improvements for wildlife came entirely from compensation for damages to wildlife by the oil companies responsible for the Santa Barbara oil spill.

I learned a lesson—that an individual really does count for something. In spite of all the anxiety about the future, and the hopeless feeling one often has regarding one's role in the face of

Even at rest, the birds tend to divide themselves into groups. When feeding, the segregation is even more pronounced, each type choosing an area suitable to its eating habits and equipment: short beaks for turning stones or packing sand; long beaks for deep mud; and medium-sized beaks for medium mud.

government and industry, individuals, by joining forces, really can be effective in making significant changes.

I don't feel proud at having declined my help back at the beginning—but I have never been happier to be wrong.

*   *   *   *

Summer was over. The shorebird season was at its peak. Thousands of birds crowded the mud flats; others waded in the shallows, while flocks of small, light-colored wings bulleted in to land and then immediately disappeared among their dun-colored brothers. Brownish bodies scurried this way and that over the mud. Heads jackhammered beaks into the ooze: long beaks, short beaks, down-curved, upswept, straight, sharp, blunt, and intermediate.

How many birds were out there? we wondered. They moved in such irregular patterns, back and forth, to and fro, that it would be impossible to count them without repeating or missing.

If a first impression gave the feeling that all of this bird activity was chaos, closer study revealed that there was a system at work. Superficially it seemed that all these birds with long legs and long bills were scrambling and competing with one another for the same food. But close watching proved that impression to be wrong. The first clue came with a study of their bills. Surely the long poker of the godwit probed for deeper organisms than the shorter bill of a willet. In fact, willets often seemed jealous of the goodies the godwits brought up from the depths of the mud, and they sometimes chased the godwits and stole their catch.

A black-bellied plover chased a fast-running isopod across the mud and grabbed it. So short bills picked at the surface.

Shoveler ducks did just what their name implies, slopping along through the softer mud at the edge of tidewater, their wide-webbed feet plopping as they walked, while avocets moved sideways through shallow water, and mallards ducked their heads for algae. Further up toward the reeds, turnstones tipped over pebbles and clam shells, grabbing isopods that had been hidden beneath.

The shorebirds were well dispersed over the mud flats segregated into different feeding zones to reduce competition between the species and provide for the best possible utilization of the food resources. We knew from what Preston Johns had told us that the ebb and flow of tidal waters brought nutrients and carried away wastes, causing a tremendous flourishing of small life. Aquatic life from the microscopic plants and animals up through hundreds or thousands of species of vertebrates and invertebrates together with their eggs and larvae: worms, clams, snails, slugs, shrimps, jellyfish, crabs, fish, isopods, amphipods, and many more.

Here, amid this busiest of bird habitats, we were reminded again of the fate that had so nearly befallen our Back Bay. We were surrounded by thousands of birds, birds that were so specialized in their ways of feeding that they could not possibly survive in any other habitat. If this "stinking slough of worthless black mud, worms, and stagnant water" (as I had once heard it referred to by a person dedicated to transforming it into residential plots), had been dredged out and channelized, changed to a marina and spiffy houses for wealthy people—where would all of these birds have gone? Wasn't it truly marvelous that a few people had spoken up and raised their voices to save the habitat?

We can never return to the Back Bay without feeling a twinge of pride and hope for ourselves and our fellows. A place like the Back Bay, a protected island of wildness in the heart of the metropolis, a place for a person to go to escape the pressures of urban life, is a treasure as much for people as for birds.

13

The Untangled Gull

We were motoring up the bay in the dory to try a little croaker fishing when we rounded the bend where we'd first seen the gull with the line and sinker. Up ahead, I spotted another gull swimming in the same area.

"I'll bet that's our friend," I said to Dad.

"Don't be silly," Dad replied. "Just because there's a gull in the same area doesn't mean it's the same gull. Besides, that's been nearly a month ago. He'd dead by now. Or maybe someone else was able to catch him and set him free."

"Just the same," I said, "I think it's him." I knew it was a million-to-one chance. But there was something about that gull . . . .

Maybe it was the labored way he was swimming, or the droopy way he was holding his wings. I'd watched the tangled gull enough times, I ought to know him when I saw him.

"Just speed up, will you?" I said. "And make a run at him. If it isn't our friend, nothing lost."

In seconds we were skimming down on the gull. We could see long before we got there that it was our friend, all right. He was swimming hard now, and any ordinary gull would long since have taken wing. As we raced down on him, he started to flap, but he wasn't having much luck getting airborne. I was sure I was finally going to get him. But somehow he did it again. At the last moment he cut back sharply and we zipped past within about a foot of being able to grab the line. Then began the old game of turning tight circles and trying to cut him off, with the gull always keeping just out of reach. I could see him pulling the same maneuver that he had used to make his escape before.

Dad did his best to keep the boat between the gull and shore, to keep him out over open water where we had our best chance of grabbing him.

After five minutes of this, it looked as though he was beginning to tire. His flights weren't so long now or so high. But we still didn't have him.

Finally he seemed to poop out all at once. He settled onto the water and swam like mad for shore. We had him at last! Still, he was a smart old gull; maybe he had another trick for us. By now nothing would surprise me. Dad eased off on the throttle and we motored up behind him slow and steady.

Then the line was ahead, cutting a V through the water, and suddenly it was simple. I just leaned over, picked up the line, and pulled it in. The line had been on him so long that it was slimy with algae.

Then I grabbed a wing and pulled him into the boat. I was bitten a few times, of course, but only hard pinches and a few scratches, nothing to worry about.

I was unwinding the tangle of monofilament from his feet when I noticed a band around one leg. There was a number stamped in the metal, and these words: NOTIFY CANADIAN WILDLIFE SERVICE, TORONTO, ONT.

We wrote down the number and let him go. He was unharmed, and without the drag of the line and weight he could fly again.

He must have been plenty glad to be rid of that sinker, which of course went immediately into my tackle box. A fair enough trade.

A couple of months after we'd sent the information to Toronto we got back a card telling us something more about our bird. This turned out to be the most curious thing about the whole episode.

Ten years ago, when I was four years old, Dad was filming a television show on Vancouver Island in Canada. One Sunday we'd taken our dory (the same one we have now) to an island where thousands of gulls nest. Dad had wanted me to see the rookery, and I was so impressed that I don't even remember it.

Anyway, according to the card we got back, our bird was a glaucous-winged gull. He had been banded when he was a baby on the very same island we had visited. We had all been on the same little island, a thousand miles away! Now here we met in the Newport Back Bay, and we saved his life. And he didn't even look back as if to say thank you.

The untangled gull, back with his flock.

You never know what goodies might be hiding under an old rusty fender. A clapper rail checks out the possibilities.

Photo Gallery

The way it was . . .

. . . and the way it is.

Until the early 1970s the upper basin of the Back Bay was sealed off into a series of shallow evaporation ponds for the extraction of salt. The only remains of this commercial enterprise is the broken-down dike that crosses the bay not far below the Interpretive Center.

The saltworks area today. One island on the site is a nesting ground for black skimmers. Newcomers to southern California, skimmers were unknown to local bird-watchers a couple of decades ago—but so were starlings, and even today's ubiquitous crows were uncommon then.

The shellmaker factory dredged the mud to extract shells of (mostly) dead mollusks. The separated mud was then piped away to deposit on the shore and islands. The shell was stockpiled before being ground into small pieces used as a calcium-rich grit additive for poultry feed.

In the old days it seemed as if about every tenth fence post was a perch for a burrowing owl. The plateaus above the Back Bay, where ground squirrels provided homes for the owls (who don't do the burrowing themselves but depend upon others to do their spade work for them), and the area around Fashion Island, were once favorite hangouts for this then plentiful species.

The road had a few rough spots before it was paved, but that only made a trip to the Back Bay something more of an adventure.

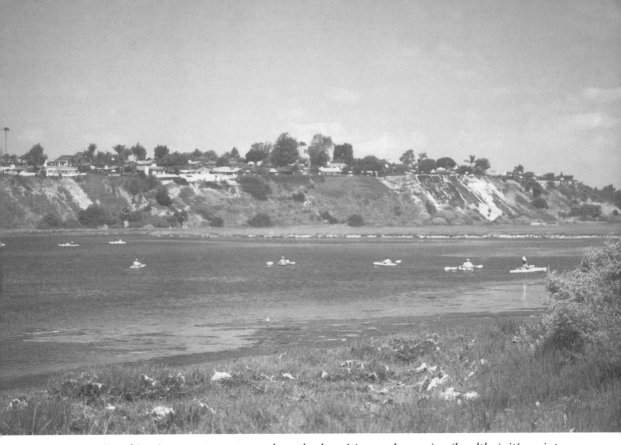

Kayaking is a great way to explore the bay. It's good exercise (healthy); it's quiet (see more wildlife); it's clean (ecologically friendly); and it's cool recreation (fun).

The bay ends at Jamboree Road. San Diego Creek, which drains many square miles of watershed, enters the bay beneath the bridge, bringing with it at every hard rain, a gillion styrofoam cups from storm drains and gutters, a few tons of silt from construction sites, gallons of dumped crankcase drainings from streets and alleys, and a flood of chemical pollutants from lawns and gardens.

Trapdoor spiders are common in the reserve but rarely seen. The catch is quick. The spider feels vibrations made by approaching prey. Then at the optimum moment she opens the door, grabs, and closes the door again in less than half a second.

Jack and Mike twenty years later.

Certificate of Appreciation

The Federal, State and Provincial Conservation Agencies join with thousands of professional and amateur ornithologists throughout North America in expressing their sincere appreciation for the interest and cooperation shown by reporting the bird band number and recovery data noted below. A report containing these data will be forwarded to the ornithologist who banded the bird and these data will be permanently retained in the cooperative North American Bird Banding files maintained at the Bird Banding Laboratory, Office of Migratory Bird Management, Laurel, Maryland 20810, U.S.A.

It is only through the continued cooperation of interested conservationists such as yourself that these important data can continue to be compiled and made available to the scientists who study our wild bird populations.

Awarded To

MIKE COUFFER
4601 SURREY DR
CORONA DEL MAR   CA   92625

BANDING DATA:

BAND NUMBER: 937-06817   KIND OF BIRD: GLAUCOUS WING GULL SEX: UNKNOWN

AGE OF BIRD: IT WAS TOO YOUNG TO FLY WHEN BANDED

BANDER: IT WAS BANDED BY PERSONNEL OF PROV MUSEUM OF BRITISH
         COLUMBIA DEPT REC & CONSV VICTORIA, B C CANADA

BANDING LOCATION: NEAR OAK BAY   B C   DATE: 07/30/74

RECOVERY DATA: FILE REF.: 20134

LOCATION: UPPER NEWPORT BAY CA   DATE: 04/26/75

CANADIAN WILDLIFE SERVICE   BUREAU OF SPORT FISHERIES AND WILDLIFE

Closure in the story of the tangled gull came with this banding report from the Canadian Wildlife Service. The gull had been ringed as a juvenile at the same rookery we visited in the dory a few years before. The bird was less than a year old when we released it from the fishing line. His or her (there's no easy way of knowing) great adventure had gone full circle with ours.

111

The Authors

Jack Couffer has had a distinguished career as a cameraman, director, producer, and writer of outstanding films and television shows. He is the author of eleven well-received books, including *Song of Wild Laughter, Bat Bomb, World War II's Other Secret Weapon,* and *The Cats of Lamu.* His previous books in the *Summer* series, published by Putnam's and co-authored with his son, Mike, are *Galapagos Summer, African Summer,* and *Canyon Summer.* He wrote, directed, and with son, Mike, did additional photography on the Upper Newport Bay Interpretive Center's show: *Salt Marsh Seasons,* a labour of love about a place close to the hearts of both men. A native Californian and a graduate of the University of Southern California, he began his career in films as a cameraman for Walt Disney in 1952. He presently divides his time between homes in Corona del Mar and Kenya.

Mike Couffer was a freshman at Corona del Mar High School when this book was written. He now pursues a love and life's work as a wildlife ecologist specializing in locating threatened and endangered species. This fuels a second passion—photography of the rare and fascinating plants, animals, and habitats with which he works.

Jacket design by Edward L. Miliano

Grey Owl Pictures, Inc.
716 Marguerite Avenue
Corona del Mar, CA 92625